# McCrae

John Bassett



Fitzhenry & Whiteside Limited

# Contents



---


195 Allstate Parkway, Markham, Ontario L3R 4T8



**The Canadians** A continuing series
*General Editor* Robert Read
*Editors* Rosalind Sharpe, Murray Lamb
*Designer* Sandi Meland

---

**Canadian Cataloguing in Publication Data**
Bassett, John M., 1920-
John McCrae

(The Canadians)

Includes index.
ISBN 0-88902-651-3

1. McCrae, John, 1872-1918. 2. Soldiers - Canada -
Biography. 3. Physicians - Canada - Biography.
I. Title. II. Series.

FC556.M42B37 1983 971.06'092'4 C83-099112-3
F1034.M42B37 1983

---

# Prologue

On a bright May morning in Belgium in 1915 a Canadian military doctor sat near the dugout that passed for his medical post. He contemplated the rows of identical white crosses in a nearby cemetery. Between the crosses, poppies had grown through the mud. It was as though the blood that had been spilled on the battlefield had been transformed into crimson flowers.

He was involved in one of the major battles of the First World War — the Second Battle of Ypres. During the prolonged engagement German troops used deadly chlorine gas as a weapon for the first time. The panic

*Portrait of McCrae by Ewan MacDonald.*

and fear it caused among the Allied troops enabled the Germans to breach the lines held by the French colonial soldiers. It was left to a handful of Canadians to hold the flank against continuous enemy offensives and shelling.

Over the preceding weeks the doctor had watched the rows of crosses lengthen daily. The most recently erected marked the grave of his close friend and former medical pupil, twenty-five year old Alexis Helmer.

It was early in the morning; the doctor had had very little sleep. He knew that at any minute more casualties would be arriving. A sense of helplessness overwhelmed him. Only a few days ago his young friend had been with him, laughing, remembering old times and planning for the future. Now, like so many thousands more, he lay dead. His grave was marked with only a plain white cross. Surely all these men had not died in vain. Would they ever *know* that their lives and courage had not been wasted? The soldier looked around him. The poppies, the budding trees, the birds' singing — all were painful reminders of more normal times and served as a searing contrast to the pain-filled reality of war that surrounded him. Resting on the back of an ambulance, he took up a pad and wrote down what he saw and felt. The result was one of the most touching and inspiring poems to be written during the First World War.

"In Flanders Fields" stirred the hearts of soldiers and their families everywhere. In simple language and with flowing sounds it vividly evoked the situation and emotions of the front-line troops. In only fifteen lines it crystallized the resolve that sustained the soldiers through the horrors of the war. It spoke of their conviction that the sacrifice of the fallen *must not* be in vain, and of the soldier's constant duty to fulfill the task begun by their dead comrades.

The poem, written in twenty minutes on the muddy fields of Flanders, is still remembered in many parts of the world. Its author was the Canadian soldier-doctor-poet, Lieutenant-Colonel John McCrae.

# The McCraes of Guelph

Chapter I

A small town in Ontario in the late 1800s was a pleasant place to grow up — especially for an energetic boy who liked the outdoors. Fish were abundant in the rivers and game was plentiful. There were acres and acres of woodland with scarcely a fence in sight, where a boy and his dog could wander freely through some of the loveliest countryside in Canada.

The town of Guelph was still quite young when John McCrae was born there on November 30, 1872. John Galt, a Scots novelist, had cut the first tree on April 23, 1827 to clear the land for what was to become today's attractive city.

John McCrae's family was also Scottish. His father came to Canada at the age of four with his parents and grandparents in 1845. The McCraes settled in Guelph and soon established themselves as respected and hardworking people. In Scotland they had been farmers. On reaching Guelph, John's grandfather, Thomas McCrae, took a job as a bookkeeper and gradually entered business on his own. He established timber mills, and later wool mills, and by 1863 he was able to move

*Guelph in the 1870s.*

*McCrae's parents, David McCrae and Janet Simpson Eckford.*

his family to their new farm, "Janefield."

Here Thomas McCrae was able to indulge his interest in livestock farming while still maintaining the family business. He soon became known over North America as a breeder of fine cattle, and his herd of prize Galloways was the finest on the continent. It was no wonder then, that his grandson developed such an affection for animals.

John's father, David, besides being an industrious businessman and cattlebreeder, was fascinated by anything military. In 1861 he organized the first Garrison Battery in Guelph to repel the Fenian Raids, and his efficiency attracted the attention of senior officers. After the Fenian episode he organized the

Ontario Field Battery which, with Colonel McCrae as Commanding Officer, won the prize for best-organized unit in the Dominion for three years in a row. He continued to hold military appointments until the outbreak of the First World War in 1914. Then, at the age of seventy-three, he organized a battery and led it to England where, to his great disappointment and annoyance, he was declared too old for service and sent back to Canada.

David McCrae instilled in his two sons, Thomas and John, a strong sense of duty and a healthy respect for military values. John, in particular, inherited his father's enthusiasm for the armed forces. He was more outgoing than his older brother, and the camaraderie, the activity and the discipline of the military life appealed to him greatly. At the age of fourteen, John joined the Guelph Highland Cadets and soon rose to the rank of lieutenant. He later joined the artillery as a gunner and eventually became a major.

*St. Andrew's Presbyterian Church, Guelph.*

As a boy John was always interested in military history and tactics. Throughout the late 1800s, the British Empire was involved in many armed conflicts with native forces of resistance, especially in India and Africa, and John read all he could about the Empire's constant military activity. He became quite knowledgeable on the subject. When he was only thirteen, he was able to spot a technical error in a well-known painting of the battle of Tel el-Kebir, while visiting an art gallery in England. This battle had taken place in 1882 in Egypt when Britain took over administration of the Suez Canal. John noticed that the artist had shown the wrong number of soldiers at each gun.

The McCraes were brought up to be religious and, as would be expected in a military family, very patriotic. Like most Scots, the McCraes were staunch Presbyterians. They were regular worshipers at St. Andrew's Presbyterian Church, never missing a Sunday service. But the McCraes did not pay attention to religion on Sunday alone; it was a part of their daily lives. Typical of nineteenth-century Presbyterians, they were well-versed in the Bible, regarding it as the only moral, social and spiritual code by which they should live. Life, for people like the McCraes, was not regarded

*University College, University of Toronto, in 1880.*

only as something to be enjoyed. It was the means by which one served God. Thus, the McCraes were taught to live strictly according to the values of hard work, self-discipline, duty and service.

As for his patriotism, John was taught to be proud not only of Canada, but of the British Empire, of which Canada was an important part. When John was growing up the Empire was at the peak of its power. It comprised a quarter of the world's population and extended to every continent and every ocean on the globe. It was natural for English-speaking Canadians like the McCraes to be imperialists. Not only were they of British origin, but Canada's membership in the Empire made her a part of the greatest power in the world, the leader of western civilization. This was a tremendous source of pride and self-confidence for the people of a still very young country.

The McCrae children were also greatly influenced by their mother, Janet Simpson Eckford, a cultured and widely-read woman who also came from a Scottish Presbyterian background. She had a sense of humour and a gift of mimicry which her son John inherited. She was also a talented musician as well as a lover of poetry. Mrs. McCrae often read poems aloud to her children and young John was spellbound by the rhythmic sounds and by the images that the words inspired. Landscapes, battles and emotions were brought to life in his mind as he listened. The poetry appealed to the thoughtful and sensitive side of John's personality. As he grew up he developed a private world of reflection and imagination that was quite different and separate from the busy world full of work, study and laughter, that he shared with his family.

One of John's distinctive qualities as a youth was his deep affection for animals. He was devoted to his family pets and horses. One winter some men saved the McCrae's dog from drowning in the river and young John soon arrived with his wagon and, wrapping the animal up in his overcoat, pulled the dog home to warm it up by the fire. All his life he felt very protective towards animals and, for some years, John's ambition was to become a veterinarian.

Although both of the McCrae boys and their sister Geills were brought up in the town of Guelph, they

*Guelph Collegiate Institute in the 19th century.*

spent a great deal of time on their grandfather's farm. The house where they were born and spent their childhood still stands. It is a comfortable home on Water Street overlooking the River Speed. It has been restored to look as it did during John McCrae's childhood, and part of it has been set aside as a museum to house McCrae family artifacts and information on his life.

The McCraes all attended public schools in Guelph. The high school that John attended, the Guelph Collegiate Institute, was small by today's standards. It had scarcely one hundred students, but it had high academic standards and it offered a suprisingly long list of subjects. There were the usual classical courses in Greek, Latin and Divinity, but what made the institute unusual was the variety of courses offered. They included such subjects as geology, physiology, optics and astronomy. Students could study the muscles, the teeth and the digestive system, or speculate on the origins of the earth.

John McCrae was an able high school student and when the University of Toronto offered him a scholarship in 1888, it seemed logical for him to pursue his interest in science and nature by studying biology there. John enjoyed his university years. He liked studying, he made many friends and he wrote a number of articles and poems for *The Varsity*, the university newspaper. One of his articles was a piece entitled "Reflections." Appearing in *The Varsity* in 1892, it described his impressions of London's Westminster Abbey, which he had visited on an earlier trip to

England. Part of the article reads:

> The spirit that can carry away from Westminster Abbey the worldly hates and petty disputings that overburdened it must lack the sensibility of its own littleness among the dust of the world's greatest . . .
>
> Heartfelt is our awe as we stand beside these lofty monuments, fit emblems of the aspirations that once warmed hearts, now forever at rest; aspirations now as lifeless as the impressive marble. Reverentially do we gaze at the tattered flags, drooping from the chancel-roof, speaking of messages from far-off fields, telling in every rent how heroes died . . .
>
> Heroes have lived and died, thrones risen and fallen, empires grown old and decayed - but through all, unchanging in their majesty, those towers have kept their watch - shone out cold and gray in the misty dawn, gleaming a reflection to the morning sun, borne unmoved the glare of the dusty noontide and faded to dark vastness in the deepening twilight.

John's years at university were marked by two difficulties. First, he suffered two serious attacks of asthma, which made breathing, and therefore studying, difficult. His asthma forced him to take a year off from his studies, delaying his graduation. Second, John could not decide on whether to be a medical doctor or a veterinarian. He knew he could only choose one career and, to help himself decide, he took time off from his studies in 1892 to become a resident master at the Ontario Agricultural College in Guelph.

His stay there was probably one of the unhappiest

*Ontario Agricultural College*

years of his life. He was unpopular with the students who apparently resented having so young an instructor. They complained about his teaching ability to the faculty, and when that brought no reaction, they threw him into a pond.

After this incident John made up his mind: he would become a doctor. At the end of the year, after a peaceful and soothing holiday on his grandfather's farm, he returned to university and graduated with an honours degree in biology in 1894. That year, John entered the Faculty of Medicine at the University of Toronto and it was immediately obvious that he had made the right decision. His marks remained consistently high and in 1898, he graduated from medical school with a gold medal for his outstanding academic performance and a scholarship in physiology and pathology.

Physiology is the study of life processes and the functions of the human body. Pathology is the study of diseases. Young Doctor McCrae decided to make his medical career in both of these fields and soon took up a posting as an intern at the Toronto General Hospital. McCrae's next appointment was in 1899 to the famous Johns Hopkins Hospital in Baltimore, Maryland. There he trained, again as an intern, under the famous Canadian physician, Sir William Osler, one of the greatest figures in modern medicine.

Osler was, among other things, a founder of modern medical education. He was one of the first to take the teaching of medicine out of the lecture hall and into the hospital wards and clinics. Under his system, which Canadian medical schools continue to use today, students became assistants to practicing doctors. They learned by doing, not just by studying. Osler also encouraged medical scholarship and taught his students to keep up-to-date with modern developments in their fields. Most important, perhaps, Sir William taught his students to treat patients as human beings who need compassion, not just as objects of medical interest.

Both John McCrae and his brother Thomas, who also took up a medical career, were tremendously influenced by Osler's teachings. They were like many promising young Canadian doctors of the time who went to Baltimore to train under Osler, usually returning to Canada to put his instruction into practice. Upon

*(top) McCrae as a university graduate (bottom) Sir William Osler.*

finishing his stint at Johns Hopkins, McCrae accepted the position of resident assistant pathologist at Montreal General Hospital, a position Osler himself had once held. He also accepted a fellowship in pathology to study at the McGill University School of Medicine. In late 1899, John moved to Montreal, planning to settle there permanently.

# War in South Africa

Chapter 2

Almost as soon as John arrived in Montreal to take up his fellowship and his residency, his career was interrupted by events taking place halfway around the world. In 1899, hostilities broke out between the Boers, farmers of Dutch origin who had settled in South Africa, and the British. The Boer-British conflict originated in the early 1800s when, at the Congress of Vienna, the Dutch colony of the Cape of Good Hope, at the southern tip of Africa, was made a part of the British Empire. Many of the Boer settlers in the colony resented

*A British cavalry patrol. Against an enemy using machine-guns, the British cavalry still fought with the lance, a weapon almost as old as warfare itself.*

being governed by the British and, in 1832, a large group emigrated to the northern region of what is now South Africa. There they established two independent republics, the Transvaal and the Orange Free State.

The British allowed the Boers to govern themselves with relatively little interference until the discovery of immense quantities of gold and diamonds in the Transvaal in the 1890s. Many British settlers from the Cape Colony, realizing the possibilities of great wealth from mining these precious minerals, emigrated to the Boer republics.

The Boers resented the British interlopers whom they called *Uitlanders* (Dutch for Outlanders.). The *Uitlanders* in turn revolted against the Boer government in 1895. Although the uprising was put down, the British pressured the Boers throughout the late 1890s to accept imperial domination of their territories. The Boers felt trapped and, in 1899, they invaded the British colony of Natal. The South African War had begun. Great Britain immediately called on Australia, New Zealand and Canada for troops and aid.

Britain's request provoked a crisis in Canada. Most English-speaking Canadians felt duty-bound to contribute to the defence of the Empire. Most French-Canadians, however, felt that the war was a foreign conflict that Canada should have no part in. Prime Minister Sir Wilfrid Laurier compromised by allowing for the establishment of a volunteer force to join the imperial army. Soon after war was declared, a small contingent of Canadian troops left for South Africa. The first contingent was too small for the large number of volunteers who still wanted to go, including the young doctor John McCrae.

Although McCrae was devoted to his medical career, he was still a military man at heart. He had been brought up to cherish the duty of fighting for one's country. Now, with the Empire threatened in one of its most important colonies, he wanted to do his part. Furthermore, McCrae had spent years in training, first as a cadet and then in the militia, and he was eager to put his military skills to the test. He had been too late in signing up for the first contingent of Canadian volunteers and when he was turned down he was bitterly disappointed. In a letter to a friend he wrote:

I see by tonight's bulletin that there is to be no second contingent. I feel sick with disappointment and do not believe that I have ever been so disappointed in my life. I am certain that there have not been fifteen minutes of my waking hour that it has not been on my mind. One campaign might cure me, but nothing else ever will. I regret bitterly that I did not enlist with the first.

In the face of war, McCrae was first a soldier; his medical career came second. "My position here," he wrote, in reference to his fellowship at McGill, "I do not count as an old boot in comparison." He wanted only to fight and he was willing to do anything to get a place in the imperial army, even if it meant going to England first. A second Canadian contingent was soon formed, however, and McCrae was accepted immediately. He arranged to have his fellowship delayed for a year and went to Guelph to join the 16th Battery, Royal Canadian Artillery. They sailed as part of the second contingent and by the beginning of 1900 he found himself in South Africa.

McCrae was attached to a field artillery unit and was soon put in charge of a section. "You have no idea of the *work*," he wrote from Cape Town. "Before proceeding to the front lines, section commanders must live with their sections, which is the right way. It makes long hours. I never knew a softer bed than the ground [on] these nights. I really enjoy every minute though there is anxiety. We have lost all our spare horses. We have only enough to turn out the battery, and no more."

Fortunately, John McCrae could usually find some amusing and interesting incident to make life more bearable. One encounter that remained vivid in his memory was his meeting with the poet and novelist Rudyard Kipling. Kipling was, at that time, at the height of his popularity. Besides being a famous, widely-read writer, he was a staunch imperialist, convinced that the British Empire was the greatest achievement of human history. It is easy to imagine the thrill that a young man would experience in having a few minutes' conversation with such a well-known man. More to the point, McCrae strongly agreed with Kipling's imperialist views, referring to the writer as "the High Priest of it all."

Whether John McCrae expected Kipling to discuss some literary topic or the greatness of the Empire is impossible to tell. All we know is that Kipling, a bit of an "armchair soldier," gave the young officer some practical advice: "Fine the men for drinking unboiled water. Don't give them CB (Confined to Barracks). It is not good. Fine them or drive common sense into them." We do not know whether McCrae followed Kipling's advice, helpful as it might have been.

McCrae had not been in South Africa for long before he became aware of the rigours of military life. It seemed that one forced march was completed just in time to set out on another. When the British troops arrived at a spot where Boer fighters were reported to be, they often found that the enemy had slipped away and another forced march had to be made. Their knowledge of the terrain and the ability to use it gave the Boers a tremendous advantage over the imperial soldiers.

In March 1900 McCrae led his troops on a 130 km march. When the British reached the enemy's location, they found that the Boers had again given them the slip. After a stop of only one day, McCrae was ordered to resume the pursuit. This entailed a march of 100 km which was to be completed in a little under thirty hours. After a very brief stop, McCrae was about to mount his horse when he found that the poor beast had fallen asleep.

John McCrae took a great interest in the well-being of all the animals used in the war. Time after time the

*Members of a Boer commando. For the Boers employed on the sieges life was fairly pleasant, since they had enough food and plenty of home leave. One of them said it was almost like being on a picnic.*

horses used in his section had to make lengthy marches and frequently they lacked the care and attention that they deserved. McCrae complained: "Everything is sent out for the 'Tommies' [British soldiers], but no one thinks of the poor horses."

Sometimes his involvement with animals had a humorous side. He describes how his horse Jack showed his mettle:

> The other day old Jack, my horse, was bitten by his next neighbour; old Jack turned slowly, eyed his opponent, shifted his rope so that he had a little more room, turned very deliberately and planted both heels in the offender's stomach. He will not be run upon.

Seeing the humour in such incidents probably helped John McCrae as much as anything to tolerate the terrible conditions of war. To a friend in England, McCrae wrote from South Africa:

> The dog is a great pleasure to have about. I think I have a personal acquaintance with them all. There are our pups. Dolly, whom I always know by her one white and black eyebrow; Grits and Tories, two smaller gentlemen about the size of a pound of butter - and fighters; one small white gentleman who rides on a horse and on a blanket. Kitty, the monkey, also rides on the forage wagon. A small shaggy chap who belongs to the Royal Irish stands on his hind legs and spars with his front feet.

*Durban Camp, South Africa, June 1902.*

There was little that was glamorous about the war in South Africa. Weather conditions often went from one extreme to the other, but McCrae realized that the human body was quite capable of adapting to the most trying circumstances when necessary. McCrae was able to tell a friend: "It is surprising how I can go without water if I have to, that is for ten hours in the sun." At the other extreme was the cold and the rain that persisted for days on end - days when it was difficult, if not impossible, to light a fire for a cup of tea.

McCrae recounted that on one occasion most of his unit's supplies went astray and he was left with only his summer gear. The transports were unable to come up with blankets and greatcoats and everyone was still soaked to the skin by the bitter cold rain. Supperless, like everyone else, McCrae managed to get some protection under an ammunition wagon. "I slept at intervals," he wrote later, "both legs in a puddle, keeping the same position all night. Ten men in the infantry regiment next to us died during the night from exposure."

*Canadians seizing a koppie (hillock) near Sunnyside during the South African War.*

Distances were so great in South Africa and the countryside so bereft of life that the British soldiers despaired of ever getting into contact with the Boers. McCrae's unit was no different from the others as it too was caught up in the ceaseless, and usually pointless, marching to and fro. The problem for the British forces was that they were using military tactics that were inadequate against the enemy they were dealing with. The Boer "commando" soldiers were engaging in guerilla warfare, hiding from the British and avoiding battles, appearing only to make sudden surprise attacks. They also knew their territory well and were skilled horsemen, which made them highly mobile. The British, on the other hand, were relatively immobile, with only ten per cent of their troops on horseback. They continued to use parade-ground tactics and rigid discipline which, while they might have been effective on European battlefields, were quite unsuitable to the rolling, desolate countryside of South Africa. The British were unable to deal effectively with an enemy like the Boers who refused to stand and fight. They were led time and again into costly and futile manoeuvres.

The British had other problems as well. Their rifles were inferior to those of the Boers and their methods were outdated; British cavalry still carried lances and swords in the first war of the twentieth century. Probably the greatest problem for the British was the incompetency of their leadership and the poor quality of their organization. Instances such as the time when McCrae's unit was deprived of its equipment were all too common among the British forces.

The result of all this was that the most powerful nation in the world took more than two years to defeat an army made up of pioneer farmers. While the British made use of 440 000 troops, the Boers could only call on 70 000 volunteer fighters. The British had more than 2000 large guns at the beginning of the war, the Boers only seventy. Most importantly, however, the Boers were fiercely determined, resourceful and dedicated to preserving their own way of life. None of these factors was true for the British.

In April of 1900 McCrae wrote: "We shall certainly have done a good march when we get to the railroad, 478 miles through a country desolate of forage, carrying our own transport. For two days running we had nine hours in the saddle without food. My throat was sore and swollen for a day or two." When McCrae wrote these words, his unit was taking part in the great march north to Pretoria, capital of the Transvaal, led by the British Commander-in-Chief Lord Roberts. It was during this advance, after weeks of marching under terrible conditions, that McCrae's unit finally made contact with the Boers. It was at Lindley in the Orange Free State, a place so small that it was rarely found on even the most detailed map. A hill of about 500 metres commanded a good view of the countryside, and the British commanders thought it should be captured. For the first few hours the British kept moving around waiting for specific orders while the Boers kept up a steady shelling of the British positions. Then a heavy fog settled in and the shelling was greatly reduced. The next morning was clear but very cold. The orders were given to advance up the steep hill. Fortunately the Boers had left during the night and the British advanced almost at will.

McCrae's account of the skirmish at Lindley is quite matter-of-fact. This might be expected as he was both an interested observer and a shrewd judge of tactics. He wrote:

> Many shells burst over and around us. We could see the smoke and the flash; then there was a soul-consuming interval of twenty to thirty seconds, when we could hear the report and about five seconds later the burst. Many in succession burst over and all around us. I picked up pieces which fell within a few feet. It was a trying afternoon and we stood around wondering. We moved the horses back and took shelter under the wagons. We were thankful when the sun went down, especially as for the last hour of daylight they turned all their guns on us. The next morning a heavy mist prevented the enemy from firing. The attack (by the British) was made in three columns. The Canadian artillery were with Hamilton's Division on the right. While we were waiting three hundred-pound shells struck the top of the ridge in succession about fifty yards in front of the battery line. The horses were put to the utmost to draw the guns up the hills. From being an infantry attack as expected it was a gunner's day and the artillery seemed to do excellent work.

On the first day of the battle the Boers on top of the ridge had been well concealed and were able to fire down on the advancing British troops. This was one of the first experiences under fire for McCrae and his men and he did not pretend that it was not frightening. He honestly admitted that "we began to feel a bit shaky." Fortunately, before the attack was mounted in full and before casualties became too serious, the Boers began to retreat. McCrae realized how serious the attack might have been. "If the enemy had had the nerve to stand", he wrote, "the Boers' position could scarcely have been taken; certainly not without the loss of thousands." A welcome order sent the troops back to camp when the British commanders realized that the Boers were leaving.

Although the South African War lasted until 1902, John McCrae returned to Canada with his unit in

*Naval guns at Bloemfontein during South African War.*

January 1901. They had signed up for only a year's service and in late 1900, after Pretoria was captured and the Boer republics dissolved, it appeared to the British High Command that the war would soon be over. Like all imperial soldiers who served in South Africa, McCrae was awarded the Queen's Medal with three clasps, one for each of the engagements in which he took part. The war continued, however, as the Boers persistently harassed the British Army in the countryside. Finally they could not hold out any longer against the sheer force of the Empire and they surrendered in 1902. The Transvaal and the Orange Free State were under British rule; the South African War was over. It had been an ominous beginning for the new twentieth century.

# Chapter 3 The Montreal Doctor

In January 1901, John McCrae returned with his unit to Canada and, after returning briefly to Guelph with the 16th Battery, went to Montreal to settle down to his medical practice and to make up for his year in South Africa. He resumed his fellowship at McGill and in a few years was lecturing in pathology at the School of Medicine. He was made pathologist at Montreal General Hospital and assistant pathologist at the Royal Victoria Hospital. In 1905 he was made a clinician at the Royal Vic, meaning a doctor who works primarily in clinics and hospital wards, and three years later was appointed to the staff of the Alexandra General Hospital as a physician.

The early years of the twentieth century were an exciting time for doctors in Canada. Medical knowledge was advancing rapidly and men like Sir William Osler were establishing an excellent reputation for the Canadian medical profession throughout western Europe and North America. John McCrae thoroughly enjoyed his career and threw himself into medical research, publishing more than forty articles between 1900 and 1914 on subjects ranging from tropical diseases to Montreal slum conditions to the detection of horsemeat in sausages. His articles were sometimes the result of laboratory research, but more often they were reports on special cases he had handled himself as a physician. Although none of his medical work revealed major discoveries, McCrae was carrying out what he saw as his duty — to contribute whatever he could to the advancement of medical knowledge.

During his years in Montreal, McCrae was influenced by another famous physician, J. George Adami. Although not as well-known as Osler, Adami was the chief pathologist at McGill Medical School and was probably the most respected pathologist in the English-speaking world. McCrae and Adami became close

friends and, eventually, co-authors. Their *Textbook of Pathology for Students of Medicine* was published in 1912 and remained a leading authority on the subject for many years.

*McCrae relaxing at his parents' home in Guelph.*

McCrae's medical reputation soon expanded outside of Montreal, even Canada itself. He was for a while lecturer in pathology at the University of Vermont and was an editor for the *American Journal of the Medical Sciences*. He was also named to the American College of

Surgeons and to Britain's Royal College of Surgeons, no mean distinction for a fairly young doctor.

While McCrae was perhaps best known as a doctor, he had other interests as well which were further developed during his years in Montreal. As we have seen, McCrae wrote a few poems while a student at the University of Toronto. It was not until he settled in Montreal, however, that he took up this activity more earnestly. McCrae was never a prolific poet. He rarely published more than two poems in one year, no doubt owing to the high standards he set for himself. Most of the poems he wrote between 1900 and 1914 appeared in the *University Magazine*, edited by his friend Andrew Macphail, another writer-doctor. Others were published in such prestigious magazines as *The Spectator, Canadian Magazine* and *The Western Minister*.

While McCrae's medical writings revealed an exact attention to detail, his poems showed him to be an imaginative and sensitive writer. Most of his poems are centred around one theme: death as an eternal rest from the trials of life. The poems generally have a depressing air about them. Perhaps this was natural, considering that McCrae's profession would have given him an acute sense of human mortality. McCrae's poems reveal a complex personality: a sensitive, melancholic soul behind the successful, accomplished physician.

One of the most interesting of McCrae's early poems was "The Unconquered Dead," written in 1905. Its concern with death, its military subject and its "voice from the grave" technique made it a forerunner of "In Flanders Fields," published ten years later.

However sombre McCrae's poems might have been he was almost always the opposite in his daily life. He smiled and laughed easily and his smile, wrote a friend, "filled the eyes and illuminated the face. It was the smile of pure fun, of pure gaiety and sincere playfulness." He was a tall, handsome man who walked," it was said, "as if he were about to dance."

His buoyant carriage and lengthy strides always attracted attention in the hospital wards he visited. McCrae had quite a temper, and he could lose it easily, expecially over examples of incompetence in his profession. But most of the time he was very good-natured and friendly, one of those people who easily

**The Unconquered Dead**

*Not we the conquered! Not to us the blame*
*Of them that flee, of them that basely yield;*
*Nor ours the shout of victory, the fame*
*Of them that vanquish in a stricken field.*

*That day of battle in the dusty heat*
*We lay and heard the bullets swish and sing*
*Like scythes amid the over-ripened wheat,*
*And we the harvest of their garnering.*

*Some yielded. No, not we! Not we, we swear*
*By these our wounds; this trench upon the hill*
*Where all the shell-strewn earth is seamed and bare,*
*Was ours to keep; and lo! we have it still.*

*We might have yielded, even we, but death*
*Came for our helper; like a sudden flood*
*The crashing darkness fell; our painful breath*
*We drew with gasps amid the choking blood.*

*The roar fell faint and farther off, and soon*
*Sank to a foolish humming in our ears,*
*Like crickets in the long, hot afternoon*
*Among the wheat fields of the olden years.*

*Before our eyes a boundless wall of red*
*Shot through by sudden streaks of jagged pain!*
*Then a slow-gathering darkness overhead*
*And rest came on us like a quiet rain.*

*Not we the conquered! Not to us the shame,*
*Who hold our earthen ramparts, nor shall cease*
*To hold them ever; victors we, who came*
*In that fierce moment to our honoured peace.*

*Stephen Leacock (1869-1944) became one of Canada's best known writers.*

inspired happiness in others.

McCrae's chief and abiding interest was people and for him, one of the great advantages of the medical profession was that it gave him the opportunity to involve himself with people from every walk of life. He especially liked children and they liked him. He could hardly pass a child in the street without stopping to strike up a conversation. In the hospital, the young patients always asked to be visited by Doctor McCrae especially. Among all the other doctors and nurses in the wards he seemed to have the greatest sympathy and understanding for children's sicknesses and problems.

There was always something very youthful about John McCrae. Not only did he look young for his age (unknowing colleagues often thought he was a medical student) but he enjoyed the company of people younger than himself. He was a very popular university lecturer; his students appreciated his dry, witty comments and his ability to explain difficult subjects clearly. He associated a great deal with other young faculty members at McGill and joined in a large number of discussion groups and clubs.

Outside of the hospital and the university, McCrae had a wide circle of friends from all sorts of backgrounds. Montreal was a much smaller city at the turn of the century than it is now and its English-speaking "society" was a closely-knit group in which McCrae was a popular figure. Everyone seemed to enjoy his company and he never lacked dinner invitations. People knew that if "Jack" McCrae was present, there was never a dull moment. He always had the right story for the right occasion and having inherited his mother's gift for mimicry and sense of humour, he could always make people laugh.

McCrae belonged to a number of professional groups, but of all of them he most deeply prized his membership in the Montreal Pen and Pencil Club. This club comprised a small group of men, whose aim was "social enjoyment and promotion of the arts and letters." Its members included men who were leading contemporary figures in Canadian arts and letters. Andrew Macphail, Stephen Leacock and even the railroad-builder Sir William Van Horne were all members.

The club used to meet regularly throughout the year with one grand annual meeting at which the first item was a handsome banquet. Afterwards the club members would examine each other's works and then read out passages from their own writings. Stephen Leacock was later to say that on these occasions McCrae's poems were greatly appreciated amidst the short stories and essays that were read out. Not only were they good, but they were short.

McCrae enjoyed his life in Montreal. Although he was unmarried, the group of young professionals that he belonged to provided mental stimulus and good company. He was a tireless worker who never refused any work that was given to him. His tasks included work in clinics, tasks in the laboratories, post-mortems, demonstrations, teaching, lecturing, visits to sick wards, reading learned papers, editing and reviewing.

John McCrae had the happy faculty of finding everything he did interesting. He especially loved to travel. He was frequently invited to the United States where he had many friends in the medical profession. When it was possible he visited Great Britain, where he had friends and relatives. One of his favourite activities in Britain was to fish for salmon in the streams of Scotland, a thrill for any dedicated fisherman. He was always an outdoorsman, enjoying camping and canoeing in the lakes of northern Canada or hiking and mountain-climbing wherever there was a hill high enough.

One of McCrae's most interesting trips was one that combined his interests in travel and in the outdoors. In 1910, he was invited on an expedition by the Governor General of Canada, Lord Grey, that went from Montreal to Prince Edward Island the long way around. The travellers headed due west from Montreal to Winnipeg. From there they turned north and canoed the Nelson River to its mouth in Hudson Bay. Then they took a steamer across the bay, headed around Labrador for the Strait of Belle Isle, passing by Newfoundland, and crossed the Gulf of St. Lawrence to their destination, Prince Edward Island. "We travelled 3000 miles," said Lord Grey after the journey, "and Jack McCrae had a story for every mile."

In 1912, John McCrae was forty years old. He had shown himself to be a man of great ability and compassion. His reputation as a doctor was well-established. He had done some writing, but hardly enough to be considered a recognized poet. He had a wide circle of friends and was a popular social figure. Though he was well-liked by his female acquaintances he was still unmarried, possibly because he was usually short of money. But it didn't look as if this situation would last much longer. By 1914, John McCrae was one of Canada's leading physicians, and it seemed as if he was finally on the verge of fame and fortune.

# The Guns of War

## Chapter 4

On a lovely June day in 1914 a young Serbian patriot assassinated the Archduke Franz Ferdinand of Austria and his wife. The murder took place in the small Balkan city of Sarajevo. Although the assassinated prince was heir to the Austrian throne, the event received very little attention in Canadian newspapers. No one could imagine that in a matter of months the murder of Franz Ferdinand would result in one of the most brutal wars in history.

For about twenty years, tensions had been developing steadily between the great powers of Europe. Great Britain, France and Germany had been competing for colonial territory throughout the world, especially in Africa. Britain and Germany had been building up powerful armies and navies in their quests for military superiority. All the leading nations were competing vigorously for economic and industrial predominance and the decaying empires, such as Austria and Turkey, were desperately holding on to their outlying territories. Furthermore, a number of extremely complex alliances had been formed between various countries as each nation attempted to seek its own interests by balancing one nation against the other. The European situation, then, was at best delicate. The assassination at Sarajevo was merely the spark igniting the conflict that became the First World War.

After the assassination, Austria declared war on Serbia. Russia then threatened war on Austria and began mobilizing its troops. Germany, which had a military pact with Austria, threatened war with Russia unless mobilization stopped. When this did not occur, Germany declared war on Russia and then on Russia's military ally, France. In order to get the first advantage, Germany invaded France by crossing through Belgium. Because Great Britain was committed to protect Belgium, it declared war on Germany. However complex were the

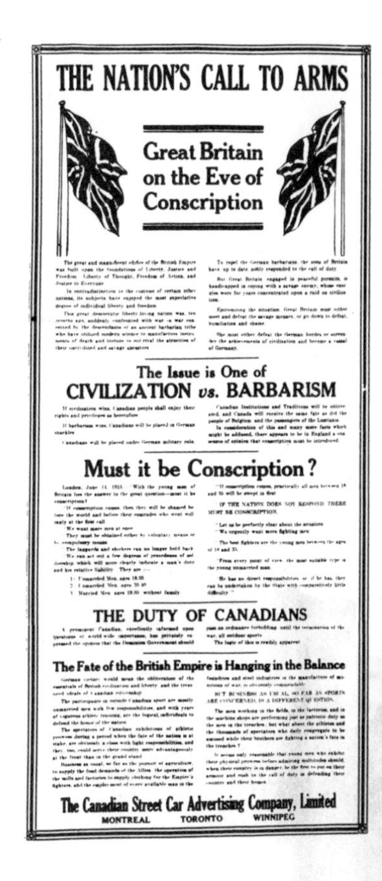
THE NATION'S CALL TO ARMS

Great Britain on the Eve of Conscription

The great and magnificent edifice of the British Empire was built upon the foundations of Liberty, Justice and Freedom. Liberty of Thought, Freedom of Action, and Justice to Everyone.

To repel the German barbarians, the sons of Britain have, up to date, nobly responded to the call of duty.

Summing the situation, Great Britain must either meet and defeat the savage menace, or go down to defeat, humiliation and shame.

She must either defeat the German hordes or surrender the achievements of civilization and become a vassal of Germany.

The Issue is One of
CIVILIZATION *vs.* BARBARISM

If civilization wins, Canadian people shall enjoy their rights and privileges as heretofore.

Canadians will be placed under German military rule.

Must it be Conscription?

IF THE NATION DOES NOT RESPOND THERE MUST BE CONSCRIPTION.

THE DUTY OF CANADIANS

The Fate of the British Empire is Hanging in the Balance

The Canadian Street Car Advertising Company, Limited
MONTREAL TORONTO WINNIPEG

*"Call to Arms" in the Globe June 17, 1915.*

beginnings of the war, it was clear that by August 1914 the great powers were ranged against one another. Germany, Austria and the Ottoman Empire (Turkey) were on one side. The Allied powers, namely France, Russia, and the British Empire, were on the other. One year later, Italy joined the Allies and in 1917, so did the United States of America. It was truly the world at war.

When Britain declared war, Canada followed suit almost immediately. As a member of the Empire, Canada's forces, like those of Australia, New Zealand and South Africa, would be a part of the British war effort. The day war was declared, John McCrae was on board a ship, bound for a holiday in England. As soon as the ship docked, he cabled back to Canada offering his services in either the artillery or the medical corps.

McCrae felt that it would be a waste of time to

*Recruiter streetcar in Toronto during World War I.*

*McCrae in military uniform.*

return to Canada, but his attempt to enlist in England was futile. After waiting almost a month he received a cablegram from his friend and former comrade in South Africa, Colonel Edward Morrison, informing him that he had been appointed surgeon to the First Brigade Artillery with the rank of major. He set sail for Canada to join the war effort that would bring him back across the Atlantic yet again in a matter of weeks.

He arrived in Montreal on September 9th with very mixed feelings. On the one hand, he felt duty-bound to do his part for his country. When war was declared there had been a surge of young men trying to enlist in Britain and Canada. They were eager to fight for King and Country and saw the coming conflict as a great

*First aid being rendered to the 5th Battalion, August 1916.*

adventure that would last only a few months. John McCrae was doubtlessly infected by the same spirit. He was still very much a military man underneath and wanted to make his contribution to the cause.

On the other hand, McCrae had been to South Africa and he knew what war meant. He had no illusions; his experience in fighting the Boers had taught him otherwise. Furthermore, he was forty-two and at his age he preferred not to be involved in the fighting. He had a well-established medical reputation in Montreal and a promising future ahead of him which the war, he knew, would ruin. All the same, he realized that he was one of the most qualified doctor-soldiers in the country and felt that it was his duty to sign up. Before leaving Montreal to go overseas, John wrote a letter to his sister Geills:

> Out on the awful old trail again! And with very mixed feelings, but some determination. I am off to Val-cartier to-night. I was really afraid to go home, for I feared it would only be harrowing for [Mother], and I think she agrees . . . . I know you will understand it is hard to go home, and perhaps easier for us all that I do not. I am in good hope of coming back soon and safely. . . .

McCrae's reasons for enlisting were typical of many young British and Canadian men. At the beginning, the war was viewed as more than just a quarrel between nations. It was the struggle between Good and Evil itself. For these men, Good was represented by the British Empire. Men like John McCrae believed that the Empire had gained control of a quarter of the globe because it represented everything that was right: justice, order and civilization. The coming war was to be more than the conquest of Germany by the Allies; it was to be the triumph of civilization, led by the British Empire, over the forces of barbarism and Evil.

Many Canadians also thought that the war would be the place where Canada could show her value to the world. More than just a junior partner in the Empire, Canada was now participating in a global event where her fighting men could have some influence on world events. Not all Canadians, however, were enthusiastic about joining the fight. As had been the case during the South African War, many French Canadians regarded the war in Europe as something foreign that did not affect Canada. Some farmers and farmers' sons were also

0.590

reluctant to fight; they did not want their livelihoods to go to ruin. Nevertheless, large numbers of young and middle-aged men like John McCrae left promising or established careers to join up with other recruits on behalf of the Empire.

Many of McCrae's friends enlisted, including fellow doctor-writer Andrew Macphail, who was over fifty and blind in one eye. Even McCrae's former teachers, Sir William Osler and J. G. Adami, both in their sixties, contributed to the military effort.

Canada as a whole contributed remarkably to the armed conflict. With a population of nearly eight million people, she was to field a force of over half a million men and women before the war's end in 1918. But the people of Canada were to pay a fearful price. Of the armed forces that went overseas, 60 000 men and women (mostly nurses) were killed and over 150 000 wounded.

In September 1914, John McCrae set off with his artillery brigade to the huge Canadian Army training camp at Valcartier, north of Quebec City. There, the entire Canadian expeditionary force was grouped and outfitted before being sent overseas. In October 1914, McCrae and his brigade sailed to England. Upon arrival, he was stationed along with the rest of the Canadian Corps in the south of the country at Salisbury Plain where the troops were trained before being sent to the front. The period at Salisbury Plain was extremely unpleasant; the rain was constant, the food poor and the organization chaotic. The Canadians were getting their first taste of war. They finally saw the real thing when they arrived at the front lines in France in February 1915.

For Major John McCrae, there were some similarities between the European war he suddenly found himself in and the war in South Africa. There were the long stretches of boredom, poor food and incompetent leadership, along with the never-ending likelihood of injury or death. On the other hand there were marked differences. In South Africa great distances had to be covered in an attempt to catch the elusive Boers, while the battle lines in the First World War were almost static for four years.

After a few months into the war, it was evident that

McCrae and horse Bonfire.

McCrae and spaniel Bonneau.

both sides had committed themselves to trench warfare. Both opponents had dug a series of trenches that stretched from the English Channel to Switzerland. In many places the trenches were only a few metres apart. Heavy rains and broken irrigation systems had turned much of the ground into muddy swamp. For four years millions of young men lived, fought, and often died in the miserable surroundings of the trenches.

It was not long before McCrae's fellow soldiers realized that the war was to be in no way a great adventure. Dreams of glory were drowned in an endless sea of mud. As the Canadian troops moved closer to the front, the signs of war steadily increased. There were more shattered houses, more shell-blasted trees, and the pools of muddy water got larger and larger. Thousands of exploding shells had churned the ground into muck. Those fortunate enough to survive spent part of the next four years living in the trenches in unimaginably horrible conditions.

During his first year at the front, McCrae had the fairly rare opportunity of being involved in both active

*A Canadian Battalion going over the top in October, 1916. Networks of trenches stretched for 950 km across France and Belgium. In some places, less than 90 m separated the opposing lines. Between these lines of trenches lay no man's land. "Over the top!" a battlefront commander would shout. Infantrymen with fixed bayonets climbed out of the trenches and dashed across no-man's land. They flung their grenades, struggled through barbed-wire entanglements and ran around gaping shell holes. Machine gun fire took a heavy toll and made successful charges almost impossible.*

and medical service. While he carried out medical duties as surgeon to the artillery brigade, he was also second-in-command to the Brigade Commander, Colonel Morrison. When he relieved the commander, McCrae was in charge of directing the fire of the sixteen and eighteen-pounder guns that constituted the unit. Often he even manned the guns himself.

Life at the front was far from pleasant for Major McCrae. One day he wrote:

Day cloudy and chilly. We wore our greatcoats most of the afternoon, and looked for bits of sunshine to get warm. About two o'clock the heavy guns gave us a 'blacksmithing.' Every time we fired we drew a perfect hornets' nest about our heads. While attending to a casualty, a shell broke through both sides of the trench, front and back, about twelve feet away. The zigzag of the trench was between it and us and we escaped. The trenches at the front were not dug in a straight line but in a zigzag pattern to prevent a large section of the trench from being destroyed. Rooms were dug into the side wall of the trenches and boards were laid down so the troops were not always standing in water. Both sides had spread huge coils of barbed wire between the trenches and had secured the coils with stakes driven into the ground. Before a soldier could cross over this "no-man's-land" the wire had to

*Taking him out on a stretcher. (5th Battalion) August, 1916.*

be cut. This could be done either at night by a soldier working in absolute darkness or by a heavy artillery barrage.

Grim as life was in the trenches, the soldiers seldom lost their senses of humour. Names were given to sections of the trenches such as Vermin Villa, The Suicide Club and The Ritz Carlton. One dugout had an elaborate sign at its entrance: "To Let. All modern conveniences including gas and water." Rest areas were located well behind the front lines. In spite of the name there was a lot that had to be done while in these areas. The soldiers had to keep up their drill, repair roads, and keep the area spotlessly clean.

Life was miserable at the front lines, even for a long-time military man like John McCrae, and throughout the war he seemed to find some sort of comfort in his affection for children and animals. Surrounded by constant destruction, McCrae appreciated the relative innocence of animals and young people. Throughout the war he wrote several letters to his nieces and nephews, giving them military ranks and promoting them from time to time. Often he wrote about two of his favourite animals, a horse called Bonfire that he had brought over from Canada and a spaniel called Bonneau. Occasionally he signed his letters with the mark of a horseshoe or a pawprint, which was supposed to be the signature of one of the animals. For instance, to his nephew, "Sergeant-Major" Jack Kilgour, he wrote:

> Did you ever have a sore hock? I have one now and Cruickshank put bandages on my leg. My master is well and the girls tell me I look well also. The ones I like best give me biscuits and sugar, and sometimes flowers.
>
> *Bonfire* *his mark.*

Many dogs followed McCrae around, but Bonneau was his favourite. Bonneau would gravely accompany him on his rounds and during McCrae's absences would sit on the road waiting for him.

It was not only the animals that McCrae was interested in. He was very concerned about the children who were victims of the war. He wrote to his niece, Margaret, about a friend of his:

> There is a little girl in this house whose name is Clothilde. She is ten years old and calls me 'Monsieur le Major.' How would you like it if twenty or thirty soldiers came along and lived in your house and put their horses in the shed. There are not many little boys or girls left in

this part of the country but occasionally one meets them on the road with baskets of eggs or loaves of bread. Most of them have no homes for their houses have been burnt by the Germans; but they do not cry over it. It is dangerous for them for a shell might hit them at any time — and it would not be an eggshell either.

Besides his friendships with his fellow soldiers, McCrae found a considerable source of moral support throughout the war in his deep Christian faith. Constantly aware of his duties as a Christian he remained a regular church-goer, often helping to lead the services when no chaplain was present. His devotion surprised a number of chaplains who were not used to such regular attendance by officers. In the years that followed, however, McCrae, like so many others, would value all the moral comfort he could get.

# Bloody Wipers Chapter 5

It was only a short time after landing in Britain before the Canadians were sent to the trenches in the region in Belguim and northern France known as Flanders. The Canadians had not yet had an opportunity to show their abilities as fighting men. As a result they were sent to a relatively quiet sector of the front called the Ypres Salient. From the very start the soldiers had difficulty with the pronunciation of Ypres (correctly pronounced "Ee-preh") so they rechristened the town "Wipers" and so it remained to the end of the war.

Until the Canadians could prove themselves as fighting men, they were regarded as troops whose primary purpose was to occupy this rather lightly-held and not very important section of the front. They could also do useful work in making the trenches more liveable

for the troops that would relieve them. The French colonial troops from Algeria who occupied the trenches to the left of the Canadians had much the same tasks.

Actually, Ypres was a town of far more importance than the High Command realized. A great many important roads ran through it and it served as a distribution centre for the area. The Ypres Salient was a semicircle of about eight kilometres. The British High Command felt that it was important for the Allies to keep control of the salient or fortification, because if it fell into the enemy's hands, movement of Allied troops from one part of the front to the other would be severely restricted. The evening of April 22, 1915 was a pleasant early spring day. There was little activity between the opposing forces. A light breeze was blowing

*The Tower, St. Martin's Cathedral, Ypres.*

*The Menin Gate at Ypres.*

from the German lines to those held by the Canadian and Algerian troops. The Allied forces were in complete ignorance of an attack that was about to be launched by the enemy against the Ypres Salient. The Germans had kept their intentions well-hidden under a cloak of security.

The first attack was directed mainly against the French colonial troops. As the Algerians waited they noticed that there was something vastly different about this attack. Carried along by the light breeze was an olive-green cloud that seemed to cling to the ground as it slowly approached the Allied forces. As it reached the Algerian and Canadian lines the soldiers realized that they were being subjected to a gas attack.

This was the first use of poisoned gas in the war. Experiments had been done with various types of gas, but at the Hague Convention before the war almost all countries had agreed never to use gas as a military weapon. The German High Command, however, felt that they should break the agreement and carried out preparations in the utmost secrecy. They had brought 5730 cylinders of chlorine gas to the front lines.

With a gentle breeze blowing on that terrible April evening, the Germans released their deadly weapon on the unsuspecting soldiers. Not knowing what to expect, the Allied troops watched the gas move towards them.

There was no protection from the chlorine which was extremely painful to breathe. It blinded the soldiers and burnt their lungs; they fell to the ground writhing and choking, many in the agonies of death. Confusion broke out. Even the horses raced about in pain. The Algerian troops fled leaving a gap six kilometres long in the trench system.

Both sides had been waiting for just such an opportunity. Now the German army had the chance to pour through the undefended lines. Not since the early days of the war had the Allies been in a more vulnerable position. For a time it seemed that nothing would or could be done to prevent the German army from advancing through the gap left by the retreating Algerian troops. No opposition appeared to exist to prevent the Allied lines from being completely shattered.

The colonial troops from Algeria could not be criticized for their actions. To stand still and to maintain their position while the deadly gas crept forward would have demanded courage of the highest order. Fortunately for the Allies, that courage was to be found in the Canadian troops who flanked the Algerians. Somehow the gap was filled; somehow the Canadian troops called on their last reserves of strength and not only stood but even managed to mount a counterattack. New as the troops were to the front lines, they stood as firm as seasoned veterans. The counterattack by the Canadians came as a complete surprise to the German commanders. The threatened breakthrough was halted.

John McCrae's post was near a particularly dangerous section of the road. The Germans had it well covered with artillery fire and for the seventeen days of the battle, McCrae saw at close view the terrible slaughter that took place. These are some of his impressions written during the two-and-a-half weeks:

This morning is the sixth day of the fight; it has been constant, except that we got a good chance to sleep for the last two nights. Our men have fought beyond praise. Canadian soldiers have set a standard for themselves which will keep posterity busy to surpass.

This is the ninth day we have stuck to the ridge, and the batteries have fought with a steadiness which is beyond all praise.

I wish I could embody on paper some of the varied sensations of that seventeen days . . . . Seventeen days of Hades! At the end of the first day if anyone had told us we had to spend seventeen days there, we would have folded our hands and said it could not be done.

The road was a nightmare to me. I saw all the tragedies of war enacted there. A wagon, or a bunch of horses, or a stray man, or a couple of men would get there just in time for a shell. One could see the absolute knockout and the obviously wounded crawling off on hands and knees; or worse yet, at night one could hear the tragedy, that horse scream, or that man's moan. Do you wonder that the road got on our nerves.

The Allied forces paid a fearful price to defend the Ypres Salient. Over 57 000 Allied troops were wounded and over 10 000 killed.

# Chapter 6 In Flanders Fields

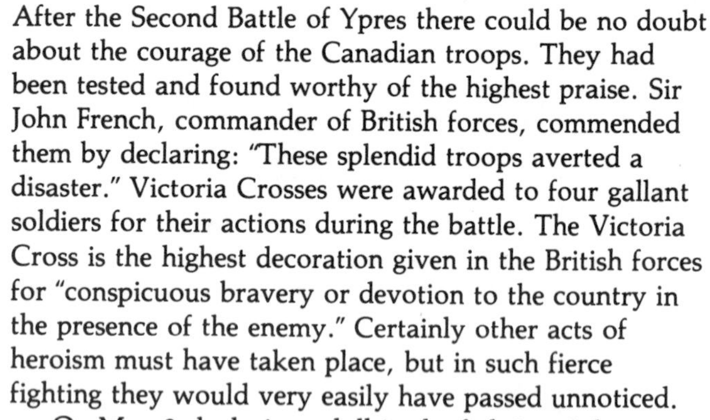

*World War I monument in Manitoba.*

After the Second Battle of Ypres there could be no doubt about the courage of the Canadian troops. They had been tested and found worthy of the highest praise. Sir John French, commander of British forces, commended them by declaring: "These splendid troops averted a disaster." Victoria Crosses were awarded to four gallant soldiers for their actions during the battle. The Victoria Cross is the highest decoration given in the British forces for "conspicuous bravery or devotion to the country in the presence of the enemy." Certainly other acts of heroism must have taken place, but in such fierce fighting they would very easily have passed unnoticed.

On May 3rd, during a lull in the fighting, John McCrae was sitting on the back of an ambulance, taking a rest from his medical duties. This dressing station was dug into the bottom of an embankment and, more than once, soldiers were shot at the top of the trench and literally rolled into the medical unit.

The day before, a former student and close friend of McCrae, Lieutenant Alexis H. Helmer of Ottawa, had been killed by a German shell. One of the most popular men in the brigade, he had died instantly, his body rendered unrecognizable. McCrae himself had performed the burial ceremony in the absence of a chaplain. It was done at night to avoid enemy detection, McCrae reciting by memory the funeral service from the Anglican prayer book.

As he sat on the ambulance, McCrae could see the cemetery where his friend was buried, a cemetery that grew day by day without pause, each grave marked by a small white cross. Since the spring weather was fast approaching, the ground was carpeted with red poppy flowers and the song of skylarks could be heard during a momentary lull in the bombardment. In a mere twenty minutes, McCrae set down his feelings in a poem.

# In Flanders Fields

—

In Flanders fields the poppies blow
Between the crosses, row on row,
That mark our place; and in the sky
The larks, still bravely singing, fly
Scarce heard amid the guns below.

We are the Dead. Short days ago
We lived, felt dawn, saw sunset glow,
Loved, and were loved, and now we lie
In Flanders fields.

Take up our quarrel with the foe:
To you from failing hands we throw
The torch; be yours to hold it high.
If ye break faith with us who die
We shall not sleep, though poppies grow
In Flanders fields

John McCrae

Punch
Dec 8·1915

**In Flanders Fields**

*In Flanders fields the poppies blow*
*Between the crosses, row on row,*
*That mark our place; and in the sky*
*The larks, still bravely singing, fly*
*Scarce heard amid the guns below.*

*We are the Dead. Short days ago*
*We lived, felt dawn, saw sunset glow,*
*Loved, and were loved, and now we lie*
*In Flanders fields.*

*Take up our quarrel with the foe:*
*To you from failing hands we throw*
*The torch; be yours to hold it high.*
*If ye break faith with us who die*
*We shall not sleep, though poppies grow*
*In Flanders fields.*

*View of cemetery McCrae was looking at when he wrote "In Flanders Fields."*

"Between the crosses, row on row.

Victory Bond poster.

There is a debate over what McCrae planned to do with the poem after he finished it. Some claim that he intended to destroy it, but was prevented from doing so only on the urging of his friends. Whatever the case, McCrae first offered "In Flanders Fields" to *The Spectator* of London, which rejected it. On December 8, 1915, it appeared in *Punch*, an English magazine devoted largely but not exclusively to humour. There was no name attached to the poem, but it did not take long for John McCrae's friends to figure out who the author was. McCrae wrote a number of copies in longhand and, as a result, minor variations appeared in some versions of the poem. Some copies have the word "grow" in place of "blow" in the first line and there were some minor differences in punctuation.

Almost immediately after "In Flanders Fields" was published it gained worldwide recognition. It struck a responsive chord in all those who were directly or indirectly involved in the war effort. For soldiers, it was an anthem of encouragement and a reminder of their duty to the dead. To those at home, it was an expression of the cause for which their country was fighting.

Soon after the poem's appearance, poppies gathered

from the battlefields of Flanders were sold in Britain to support war expenses. The poppy became a symbol of the Allied war effort and of the soldiers who had died in its cause. After the war, the American and Canadian Legions adopted the poppy as a symbol of remembrance and sacrifice. The poppies we buy every November 11th were inspired by McCrae's famous poem.

The spirit of "In Flanders Fields" was not felt in English-speaking countries alone. It was translated in several languages, to the point where McCrae himself once remarked, "It needs only Chinese now, surely." The poem obviously had a universal appeal. Its message could be understood by people of almost all nationalities. One of the first of many translations of the poem was by Maurice Glorion into French. It reads:

**Quelque Part en Flandre**

*En Flandre, quelque part sur un champ de bataille,*
*Entre nos croix de bois ont fleuri les pavots.*
*Dans le ciel, ignorant le bruit de la mitraille,*
*L'alouette gaiement chante le jour nouveau.*

*Nous, les morts d'aujourd'hui, vivants hier encore,*
*Nous riions, nous aimions et nous étions aimés;*
*Nous, dont les yeux voyaient le couchant et l'aurore*
*En Flandre, quelque part, reposons à jamais.*

*Vous qui survivez, c'est à vous de répondre*
*La flambeau du combat dans nos doigts décharnés.*
*C'est un devoir sacré. Sous la terre de Flandre,*
*Nous ne dormirons point si vous le prafanez.*

McCrae's poem also prompted many replies. One of the best is the poem of an American, R. W. Lilliard. Entitled "America's Answer," it reads:

*Rest ye in peace, ye Flanders' dead,*
*The fight that ye so bravely led*
*We've taken up. And we will keep*
*True faith with you who lie asleep.*
*With each a cross to mark his bed*
*And poppies blowing overhead*
*Where once his own life blood ran red;*
*So let your rest be sweet and deep,*
*In Flanders Fields.*

*Fear not that ye have died for naught;*
*The torch ye threw to us we caught,*
*Ten million hands will hold it high,*
*And Freedom's light shall never die!*
*We've learned the lesson that ye taught*
*In Flanders Fields.*

While "In Flanders Fields" was probably the most popular poem to come out of the war, John McCrae was only one of a number of celebrated soldier-poets to write about the conflict. Great Britain, especially, produced a large number of war-poets whose works also remain significant and widely read. Men like Rupert Brooke, Siegried Sassoon and Wilfred Owen vividly portrayed the various sentiments that characterized the First World War: the thrill of enlistment, the drudgery of army life, the horror of warfare and the fear of death. "In Flanders Fields" was an important Canadian contribution to one of the most distinctive literary forms of the twentieth century, the literature of war.

# Chapter 7 Behind the Lines

*29th Infantry Battalion advancing over "No Man's Land" through the German barbed wire and heavy fire at Vimy Ridge, April, 1917.*

"In Flanders Fields" was written in early May of 1915 and McCrae remained stationed at the front for another month. His letters were filled with references to the constant activity. May 3rd: "A clear morning, and the accursed German aeroplanes are over our positions again." May 5th: "Heavily hammered in the morning from 7 to 9; but at 9 it let up; the sun came out and things looked better." May 8th: "The whole front is constantly ablaze with big gunfire; the racket never ceases . . . . You may imagine our state of mind, unable to get anything sure in the uncertainty, except that we should stick it out as the guns would fire, and we could fire them." On May 10th, he wrote as the battle of Ypres was letting up:

> The general impression is a nightmare. We have been in the most bitter of fights. For seventeen days and seventeen nights none of us has had our clothes off. In all the time I was awake gun or rifle fire never ceased for sixty seconds . . . . I have done what fell to hand. My clothes, boots, kit and dugout at various times were sadly bloody. We have constant, accurate shell fire but we have given back no less.

On June 1, 1915, John McCrae was transferred from the front and made Lieutenant-Colonel in charge of medicine at No. 3, Canadian General Hospital (McGill) at Boulogne, France. Despite his promotion, McCrae was furious. He felt more like a soldier than a doctor and he felt that his place was with the guns. "All the doctors in the world won't win this war," he said angrily. "What we need is more fighting men." In a more subdued tone, he wrote to his mother:

> We were all sorry to part . . . friendships under these circumstances are apt to be the real thing. I am sorry to leave them in such a hot corner, but cannot choose and must obey orders. It is a great relief from strain, I must admit, to be out, but I could wish that they all were.

At his new posting McCrae worked hard, as he did in any task. At first he missed being at the front. "I expect to wish often that I had stuck by the artillery," he wrote. Always eager and adventurous he missed the action of the front lines. He also had contempt for "non-combatant" military service, not realizing that in modern warfare the medical service was quite dangerous because of its immobility and its vulnerability under attack. McCrae was soon to find that there was no shortage of

work at the Boulogne Hospital. For the next two-and-a-half years he had increasing numbers of casualties to attend to, as the war seemed to continue without end.

During those two-and-a-half years the men of the Canadian Corps were involved in a large number of battles, distinguishing themselves as they had done at the Second Battle of Ypres. During that time, despite valiant effort, they only made relatively insignificant gains. The Canadians finally achieved a significant victory on April 9, 1917 with the capture of Vimy Ridge. Four attempts by the British and French had failed to dislodge the Germans from this key stronghold and when the Canadians finally took Vimy it was, until then, the greatest Allied victory of the war.

The taking of Vimy Ridge established the military reputation of Canadian troops, but it did not mean the end of the war. In July 1917, the Canadians were called upon to take part in one of the bloodiest conflicts of the war, the Battle of Passchendaele. During the month of August four million British shells pounded the German defences, destroying the centuries-old series of dykes and canals that protected the Belgian village of Passchendaele

*Wounded Canadians en route for Blighty.*

*A badly wounded Canadian being carried to aid post by German prisoners.*

from the sea. The area became a dangerous wasteland of mud. Tanks and other vehicles became useless and soldiers who fell off the wooden duckboards often drowned, swallowed up by the swamp.

When the Canadian Corps, now commanded by the Canadian-born General Sir Arthur Currie, moved in to take Passchendaele in the fall of 1917, the casualties were enormous. Not only did soldiers fall victim to German air attacks and mustard gas, but soldiers drowned in the mud or contracted diseases resulting from the horrific living conditions. Bodies could not be buried in the mud. Water had to be transported in gasoline tanks. Death, sickness and rats were everywhere. After an extraordinary effort Passschendaele

Ridge was finally captured in November 1917 at the cost of 16 000 Canadian casualties.

Treating the seemingly endless stream of wounded who were brought into the hospital at Boulogne began to take its toll on John McCrae. He had signed up for the war expecting to return to Montreal in a matter of months. He had always been optimistic about the chances of Allied victory and enthusiastic about doing his part. By November 1917, however, his characteristic air of jaunty assurance had disappeared. Three long years of war had changed John McCrae.

Far from the friendly, smiling man who had been the charm of Montreal society, McCrae had become a sullen man of few words. Always a strict disciplinarian, in the later years of the war he began to lose his temper easily and to use harsh words with his subordinates. He was still admired by his staff, but it seemed as if he was happiest when he was riding alone on his horse, Bonfire. Indeed, as McCrae became more detached from people, he became more attached to his dog Bonneau, who

*A bayonet, scabbard and entrenching tool handle were used as splints on the arm of this Canadian soldier whose upper arm was broken by a piece of shrapnel.*

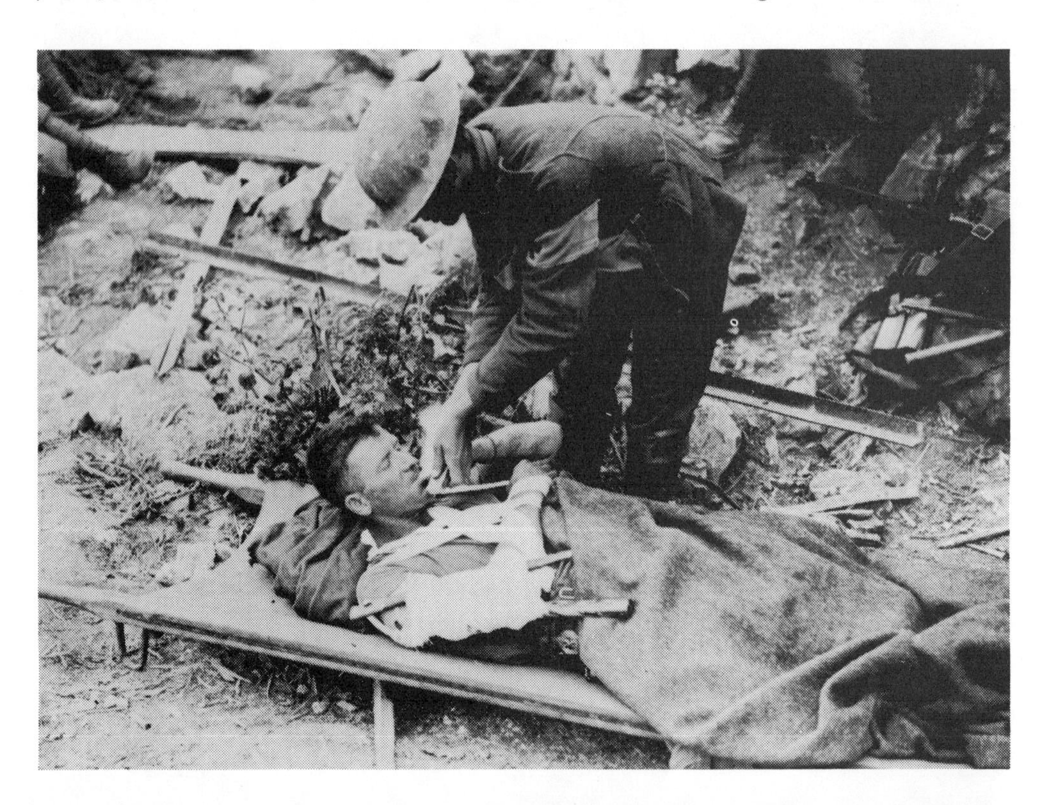

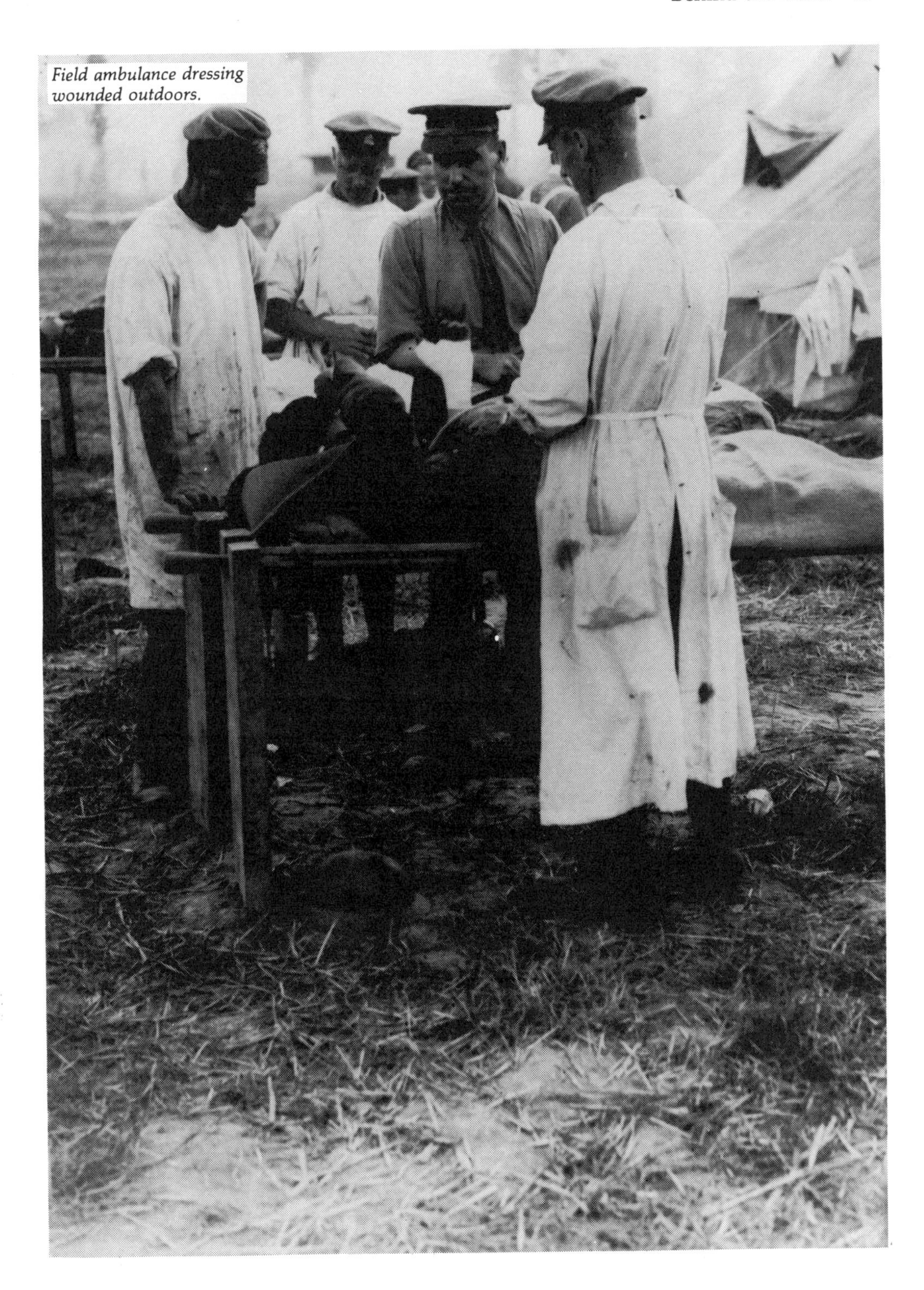

*Field ambulance dressing wounded outdoors.*

faithfully continued to follow McCrae around the wards, and to his horse. "I have a very deep affection for Bonfire," he wrote, "for we have been through so much together, and some of it bad enough. All the hard spots to which one's memory turns the old fellow has shared, though he says so little about it."

From the Second Battle of Ypres to the Battle of Passchendaele, McCrae had seen many friends and acquaintances dead or wounded, and it never seemed to stop. For three years, the Allies had been battering the enemy, inflicting and suffering huge numbers of casualties, all for a few kilometres of mud. For McCrae, the war was turning into a failure of the power and ideals of the British Empire, rather than the triumph he had expected. McCrae had dedicated himself to a cause which he thought was right and just, and after three years of poor leadership, inhuman slaughter and widespread destruction, his cause seemed further away from victory than ever.

The other source of frustration for McCrae was his relegation to the rear lines of battle. He had been brought up on a tradition of military duty and service; he was first and foremost a soldier, a fighting man. For him the real fight was in the front lines with the guns. He felt that by serving with the medical corps he was not truly doing his part. Away from the front he felt that he was letting down his comrades; they were dying and suffering while he was living in comparative safety.

In November 1917, a nursing sister who had known McCrae for some years met him while he was on leave in France and at first failed to recognize him. She had known a handsome, lively charming officer who warmed the heart of everyone he met. She saw before her now a face lined and ashen grey, a man whose movements were slow and heavy. His other friends noticed that even more than his former cheerful appearance, McCrae had lost his spirit. He was a broken man.

# Short Days Ago Chapter 8

The winter of 1917 was a particularly cold one in western Europe and McCrae, who was growing worn, tired and asthmatic, felt it noticeably. In January he wrote:

> The cruel cold is still holding. Everyone is suffering and the men in the wards in bed cannot keep warm . . . . For my own part I do not think I have ever been more uncomfortable. Everything is so cold that it hurts to pick it up. To go to bed is a nightmare and to get up a worse one. I have heard of cold weather in Europe, and how the poor suffer, — now I know!

On January 13, 1918, Lieutenant-Colonel John McCrae's dedication and hard work at the Boulogne hospital was rewarded. That day he was notified of his appointment to the position of Consulting Physician to the British Armies in France, with the temporary rank of Colonel. This made McCrae one of the chief medical officers in the British forces, a well-deserved distinction. His ability as a clinical physician and pathologist had

*McCrae's funeral. General Currie and General Morrison standing in front of "Bonfire."*

made him an effective wartime medical officer. One of his colleagues at Boulogne, Colonel Elder, later wrote that McCrae "was very much pleased with the appointment. We discussed the matter at length and I took his advice upon measures for carrying on the medical work of the unit."

That same day, however, McCrae complained of a slight headache. He confined himself to his quarters but by nightfall was feeling worse. He realized the next day that he had contracted pneumonia. He was removed to the officers' hospital at Wimereux, France, but his condition deteriorated steadily. He had also contracted cerebral meningitis and soon lapsed into a coma, and on January 28, 1918, exhausted after years of overwork, John McCrae died.

His funeral was held at the military cemetery at Wimereux and was attended by military personnel of all ranks. Lieutenant-General Sir Arthur Currie, Commander of the Canadian Corps, was present, as was General Edward Morrison, McCrae's friend and former comrade in the artillery. A hundred nursing sisters in cap and veil also attended. Years later, one of them wrote: "The nurses lamented that he became unconscious so quickly they could not tell him how much they cared. To the funeral all came as we did, because we loved him so." The casket, draped with the flag and with McCrae's cap on top, was carried to the cemetery on a gun carriage, his horse Bonfire being led behind. The firing squad that usually accompanies military funerals went through the motions but did not fire, because the cemetery was in the war zone. The service was read and Lieutenant-Colonel John McCrae was buried "on a sunny slope facing the sunset and the sea."

John McCrae was mourned by a multitude of people who had been inspired by "In Flanders Fields". To the families of the fallen especially, he had given a message of comfort and hope. Now with his own death, McCrae's poem was even more poignant. As far as we know, McCrae wrote only one poem after "In Flanders Fields". Entitled "The Anxious Dead", it reflects the same theme as the more famous poem, namely that the living have a duty to avenge those who died for them. Two of the poem's verses read:

*O guns, fall silent till the dead men hear*
*Above their heads the legions pressing on.*
*They fought their fight in time of bitter fear*
*And died not knowing how the day had gone.*

*Tell them, O guns, that we have heard their call,*
*That we have sworn and will not turn aside,*
*That we will onward till we win or fall.*
*That we will keep the faith for which they died.*

The death of John McCrae was only one among the hundreds of thousands of casualties of the First World War. In a four-year struggle that had seen the horrors of trench warfare, gas attacks, widespread destruction and extraordinary losses of life, the death of one Canadian officer was hardly noticeable. Yet, in many ways, John McCrae represented much of the spirit that kept the men fighting between 1914 and 1918. He firmly believed in the cause he was fighting for, and his sense of duty to Canada and to the Empire never weakened. He was also first and foremost a soldier, and whether manning the guns, tending the wounded or helping to lead in the prayers he felt a strong bond of service and friendship towards his comrades in arms. It was for them that he had written his poem; it was for them that he had done his part in the war.

Like so many other people cut down in their prime, John McCrae was remembered by his friends not only for what he had accomplished, but for what he might have done. McCrae's friend and colleague at McGill,

Professor Stephen Leacock, probably wrote as good an epitaph as any when he later praised McCrae for " . . . his vitality and splendid vigour, his career and honour and marked distinction, his life filled with honourable endeavour and instinct with a sense of duty." At the medical school of McGill University, a window commemmorates John McCrae with this simple description: "Pathologist, Poet, Soldier, Physician, Man Among Men."

# Index





# Credits

The publishers are grateful to the following for illustrations:
City of Toronto Archives, page 30
Colonel John McCrae Birthplace Society, pages 3, 6, 11 (top), 23, 31, 35, 47, 48, 49, 59,
Guelph Civic Museum, pages 1, 7, 9, 10
Manitoba Archives, page 46
Metropolitan Toronto Library Board, pages 13, 16
National Library, page 29(8208)
The Public Archives of Canada, pages 11(PA 7105), 17(CPA 16430), 18(PA 15300), 20(PA 6400), 25(PA 1879), 26(PA 110154), 33(PA 794), 36-37(PA 648), 38(PA 518), 42(PA 329), 43(PA 4618), 52-53(PA 1086), 54(PA 1679), 55(PA 1601), 56(PA 3217), 57(PA 2890)

Every effort has been made to credit all sources correctly. The author and publishers will welcome any information that will allow them to correct any errors and omissions.